My First Acrostic

The South

Edited by Claire Tupholme

First published in Great Britain in 2010 by:

Young Writers
Remus House
Coltsfoot Drive
Peterborough
PE2 9JX
Telephone: 01733 890066
Website: www.youngwriters.co.uk

All Rights Reserved
© Copyright Contributors 2009
SB ISBN 978-1-84924-736-8

Foreword

The 'My First Acrostic' collection was developed by Young Writers specifically for Key Stage 1 children. The poetic form is simple, fun and gives the young poet a guideline to shape their ideas, yet at the same time leaves room for their imagination and creativity to begin to blossom.

Due to the young age of the entrants we have enjoyed rewarding their effort by including as many of the poems as possible. Our hope is that seeing their work in print will encourage the children to grow and develop their writing skills to become our poets of tomorrow.

Young Writers has been publishing children's poetry for over 19 years. Our aim is to nurture creativity in our children and young adults, to give them an interest in poetry and an outlet to express themselves. This latest collection will act as a milestone for the young poets and one that will be enjoyable to revisit again and again.

Contents

Athelstan House School, Hampton
Finn O'Brien (6) 1
Read Fuller (6) 1
Hallam Radley (6) 1
Nikhil Halwasiya (7) 2
Sam Bullen (6) 2
Lauren Cunningham (6) 2
Arran McFarlane (6) 3
Joshua Peachey (6) 3
Rory Cunningham (6) 3

Badgemore Primary School, Henley on Thames
Jasem Ferjani (6) 4
Dominique McLean (6) 4
Lucia Mora Urbina (6) 5
Harrison McLean (6) 5
Libby Hooper (5) 6
Ben Few (6) 6
Kyle Hatch (6) 6

Bushey Heath Primary School, Bushey Heath
Maddison Heyler (6) 7
Cameron Bamberg (6) 7
Kai Jackman (6) 7
Jackson Helyer (6) 8
Alysha Khan (6) 8
Calum Hart (6) 8
Nicole Redmond (6) 9
Joseph Kabel (7) 9
Aaryan Sheth (7) 9
Danny Lawrence (6) 10
Holly French (6) 10
Poppy Ainslie (7) 10
Ethan Bradley (6) 11
Jack James (6) 11
Anna Finley (6) 11
Ben Fullman (7) 12

Castle Hill Infant School, Basingstoke
Mya O'Grady (7) 12
Isabel Tarry (6) 12

Katherine Monk (6) 13
Keeleigh Vint (6) 13
Jessica Gillman (6) 14
Parnika Agrawal (6) 14
Erin Riggall (6) 14
Shannon Crawford (6) 15
Rebecca Dark (6) 15
Toby Micallef (6) 15
Charlie Pergusey (7) 16
William Browne (7) 16
Ella Bennett (6) 16
Bradley Clarke (7) 17
Hannah Chamberlain (6) 17
Libby Bonner (7) 17
Abitha Nanthakumar (6) 18
Joshua Challis (6) 18
Sophie Murray-Cousens (7) 18
Connor Richardson (6) 19
Harley Bateman (6) 19
Simran Atwal (6) 19
Hannah Rogers-Mitchell (6) 20
Kieran Davidson-Blake (6) 20
Joshua Allen (6) 20
Connor Solley-Andrews (6) 21
Milly Toombes (6) 21
Lexie King (6) 21
Mason Knott (6) 22
James Lyness (7) 22
Aryun Banga (6) 22
Harry Wells (6) 23
Craig Stock (6) 23
Lewis Hall (7) 23
Renee Mhuri (6) 24
Ryan Lock (6) 24

Chilworth CE Aided Infant School, Chilworth
Max Carvalho (6) 24
James Jenkins (6) 25
Ewa Borzecka (7) 25
Daisy Dunne (6) 26
Joshua Ingham (6) 26
Sian Gillingham (6) 27

Connie Sharp (6) 27
Rosie Savage (6) 27
Toby Brewer (6) 28
Jemma Ellis (6) 28
George Summerfield-Scott (6) 28
Amelie Butler (6) 29
James Kinton (6) 29

Edward Betham CE Primary School, Greenford
Harry Duffy (6) 29
Laura Eshun (6) 30
David Morohunfola (7) 30
Cerys McNeil (7) 31
Jhokasta Candelas (6) 31
Isabel Hunte-Wood (6) 32
Joshua Grant-McKenzie (7) 32
Mia Thomas (7) 33
Hailey Sathyavan (6) 33
Hazel Sathyavan (6) 34
Semra Karakaya (6) 34
Adrine Andreasian (6) 35
Sophie Tebbit (6) 35
Robbie Blair (6) 36
David Akinwande (7) 36
Frankie Snell (6) 37
Kyza Tettey (6) 38
Jack O'Gara (6) 38
Lydia Malecaut (6) 39
Pierre Metry (7) 39
Dante George (6) 40
Adam Hayward (6) 40

Farleigh School, Andover
Frederick Falk (6) 41
Lara Smyth-Osbourne (6) 42
Angus Mihell (6) 42
James Hayes (7) 43
Ed Betton (6) 43
Holly Bentley (7) 44
Saffron Davie-Thornhill (6) 44
Amelia Ursell (6) 45
Sebastian Kilpatrick (6) 45
Amelie Osborn-Smith (6) 46
Charlie MacDonald-Smith (6) 46
Thomas Harvie-Watt (6) 47
William Marsh (6) 47

Béla Jankovich Besan (6) 47

Foxmoor School, Stroud
Michael Crilley (6) 48
Ben Brown (6) 48
Bryony Buckland (6) 49
Phoenix Dangerfield (6) 49
Charlie Pearce (7) 50
Maisey Hammond (6) 50
Zack Eckersall (6) 51
Tiarna Crowther (6) 51
Tom Pickering (6) 52
Ellis Heath (6) 52
Iwan Rossiter (6) 53
Beth Fowles (6) 53
Mia Gardener (6) 54
Alice Hill (6) 54

Harlyn Primary School, Pinner
Alex Bennett (6) 55
Lucy Sutch (6) 55
Sophia Kerridge (6) 56
Amba Mehta (5) 56
Ethan Crockford (6) 57
Eloise Curtis (5) 57
Sophie Jenkins (6) 57
Emily Barnard (6) 58
Ashwin Sangarpaul (5) 58
Jasmine Tailor (6) 58

Holy Apostles CE Primary School, Cheltenham
Blake Penwarden (6) 59
Jack Wilkins (6) 59
Jacob Adams (7) 60
Faneem Mansoon (6) 60
Leo Daubeney (6) 60
Sophie Cole (6) 61
Sam Seeley (6) 61

Holy Family RC Primary School, London
Cameron Carlton (7) 61
Maisie Sykes (7) 62
John Sawyer (6) 62
William Li (7) 63
Daniel Li Nguyen (5) 63
Grace Beautyman (6) 63

Serena Hapurachilagai (7) 64
Ermias Wondwossen Hailu (7) 64
Azaria Kidane (6) 64
Leah Ellie Wren (6) 65
Lashae Julius (6) 65
Joseph Davies (7) 65
Megan Rafat (6) 66
Demi Mifsud (6) 66
Ronnie Heavey (6) 66
Bolu Shobowale (6) 67
Renee Palmer (6) 67

Lime Walk Primary School, Hemel Hempstead
Rosie Farney (6) 67
Tobi Pocock (6) 68
Kai Gordon (6) 68
Jake Final (6) 68
Josh King (6) 69
Hannah Nicholson (6) 69
Luke Thomas (6) 70
Thomas Borrowdale (6) 70
Mehrin Ahmed (6) 71
Luke Jenkins (6) 71
Kazie Dufaur-Green (6) 71

Ramsey Manor Lower School, Barton Le Clay
Sky Cassels (6) 72
Ciaran Moore (6) 72
Holly Brennan (6) 73
Ella Revels (6) 73
Courtney Rogers (6) 74
Joseph Edmunds (6) 74
Tilly Haestier (6) 75
Abigail Green (6) 75
Kate Kilby (6) 76
Finlay Dolan (6) 76
Isobel Marshall (6) 77
Sam Dreyer (6) 77
Ben Miller (6) 78
Adam Mann (7) 78
Leanne Day (6) 79
Georgia Philpot (6) 79
Ellie Bromhall (6) 79
Chloe Burr (6) 80
Oliver Mann (6) 80

Ben S Smart (6) 80
Ben O Smart (6) 81
Aneesa Qurban (6) 81
Joshua Webster (6) 81
Oliver Holder (6) 82
Blayn Gill (7) 82
Ava Powell (6) 82
Taylor Watson (7) 83
Abbie Giles (6) 83
Milly Heys (6) 83
Joseph Holloway (6) 84
Beau Garner (6) 84
Jonah Barton (6) 84
Lauren Elliott (7) 85
Hannah Dixon (6) 85
Eleanor Hoyle (6) 85
Euan Randall (6) 86
Jessica Woods (6) 86
Sophie Bishop (7) 86
Elise Rennie (6) 87
Grace Hattle (6) 87

St Winifred's School, Portswood
Nathalia Clark (7) 87
Alistair Howard (5) 88
Ruggero Ullan Pastore (5) 88
Ankit Nambiar (6) 89
Naomi Collymore (5) 89

Shoreham College, Shoreham by Sea
Dominic Chatterton-Sim (7) 89
Llewellyn Jones (6) 90
Mackenzie Cannon (6) 90
William Huet (6) 91
Thomas Wootton (6) 91
Sydney Gillman (6) 92
Joseph Ainsworth (6) 92
Joshua Stearns (6) 92

The Christian School, Takeley
Roseanna Davey (6) 93
Rachel Fyfe (6) 93

Trotts Hill Primary School, Stevenage
Ella-Mae Sinkia (6) 93

**Tylers Green First School,
High Wycombe**
Ella Upcraft (6) 94
**Whalton CE Aided First School,
Morpeth**
Will Redmayne (7) 94

The Poems

My First Acrostic - The South

Gorilla

G reedy
O ver the trees they go
R eally big
I like bananas
L arge
L eap from branch to branch
A ngry.

Finn O'Brien (6)
Athelstan House School, Hampton

Giraffe

G entle as a dog
I t lives in Africa
R uns very fast
A giraffe's neck is long
F eels soft
F eeds on leaves
E ach giraffe has dots.

Read Fuller (6)
Athelstan House School, Hampton

Lion

L arge as a dragon
I t lives in the jungle
O n the plain
N ear a cave.

Hallam Radley (6)
Athelstan House School, Hampton

Nikhil

N ice
I am a boy
K ind
H appy
I like school
L augh all the time.

Nikhil Halwasiya (7)
Athelstan House School, Hampton

Dragon

D angerous as a lion
R oars loudly
A nd eats buffaloes
G reat big teeth
O n its back are scales
N othing can kill it.

Sam Bullen (6)
Athelstan House School, Hampton

Horse

H appy as a smiley baby
O beyed
R uns in a race
S mells like a pig
E yes are blue.

Lauren Cunningham (6)
Athelstan House School, Hampton

My First Acrostic - The South

Bull

B ig as my school
U gly as a pig
L ooks big
L ies in the fields.

Arran McFarlane (6)
Athelstan House School, Hampton

Cat

C limbs a tree
A nd fights with sharp claws fiercely
T iny cats are called kittens.

Joshua Peachey (6)
Athelstan House School, Hampton

Dog

D og that digs for bones
O r runs in the park
G rowls at cats.

Rory Cunningham (6)
Athelstan House School, Hampton

Harvest

H ot like the sun
A ll the sun makes you sweat
R adishes small like sweets
V egetables so delicious
E lephant is so big
S heep are so fluffy
T ractor is so big.

Jasem Ferjani (6)
Badgemore Primary School, Henley on Thames

Harvest

H ungry
A pples are like roses
R oses are like flowers
V egetables are in harvest time
E vyerone likes harvest
S weet apples are red
T reasure swaying in the harvest.

Dominique McLean (6)
Badgemore Primary School, Henley on Thames

My First Acrostic - The South

Harvest Festival

H arvest is fun like a fair
A pples grow in harvest
R ibbons are nice in harvest
V eggies are kind of harvesty
E veryone likes harvest
S carecrows are scary in harvest
T rees are nice in harvest.

Lucia Mora Urbina (6)
Badgemore Primary School, Henley on Thames

Harvest

H arvest festival
A mazing like a fair
R ed leaves fall off the tree
V egetables
E xcellent
S unny like a rainbow
T ractors cut the wheat.

Harrison McLean (6)
Badgemore Primary School, Henley on Thames

Seeds Growing

S eeds growing underground
E veryone is growing flowers
E veryone tries to grow fruit
D ig them up and plant them down
S eeds growing underground.

Libby Hooper (5)
Badgemore Primary School, Henley on Thames

Farming

F ruit
A pples growing
R abbits
M elons
S heep.

Ben Few (6)
Badgemore Primary School, Henley on Thames

Farming

F un
A pples
R ory
M um
S nake.

Kyle Hatch (6)
Badgemore Primary School, Henley on Thames

My First Acrostic – The South

Maddison

M arshmallows are my favourite
A puppy is a nice pet
D ogs are my best pets
D uffels is my friendly puppy
I s nice to have summer
S unshine is bright
O n camping days it is fun
N ice friends are lovely.

Maddison Heyler (6)
Bushey Heath Primary School, Bushey Heath

I Like Cars

C ars are things I like
A nd Black-Eyed Peas, Lily Allen and Lady GaGa too
M y best TV show is 'How It's Made'
E ggs are food I like best. Frogs are my best animal
R ibbit, I like the noise, ribbit for a frog
O n a go-kart it's not nice, it's fast too
N ow is a word I like.

Cameron Bamberg (6)
Bushey Heath Primary School, Bushey Heath

Kai

K icking a ball is fun
A pples are nice
I like TV.

Kai Jackman (6)
Bushey Heath Primary School, Bushey Heath

Jackson

J elly is my favourite food
A pples are fruit
C urry is my favourite dinner
K it is my favourite toy
S inging is what I like to do
O ranges are my favourite fruit
N oisy toys are my favourite toys.

Jackson Helyer (6)
Bushey Heath Primary School, Bushey Heath

Alysha

A pples are my favourite
L ava is scary
Y ou give me treats
S nakes are my favourite
H ard stuff is not my favourite
A nd ice cream is yummy.

Alysha Khan (6)
Bushey Heath Primary School, Bushey Heath

Untitled

C alum likes chewing gum
A pril is my birthday month
L ara is my friend
U mbrella is my raincoat
M addison is my friend.

Calum Hart (6)
Bushey Heath Primary School, Bushey Heath

My First Acrostic - The South

Nicole

N ight-time goes past
I am good at dancing
C ats are my second favourite
O pen the door for me please
L ike to play with my puppy
E very one so nice.

Nicole Redmond (6)
Bushey Heath Primary School, Bushey Heath

Joseph

J uices I like
O range is my favourite fruit
S harks I like
E lectronics I like
P igs I don't like
H olly F, she likes me.

Joseph Kabel (7)
Bushey Heath Primary School, Bushey Heath

Aaryan

A pple juice is my best drink
A nd pizza is my favourite food
R unning pretty fast is hard
Y ellow is a horrible colour
A nd pink even worse
N ails normally kept quite short.

Aaryan Sheth (7)
Bushey Heath Primary School, Bushey Heath

Danny

D ogs are my favourite animal
A pples are my best fruit
N uts are nice
N utcrackers are nice
Y oghurt is yummy.

Danny Lawrence (6)
Bushey Heath Primary School, Bushey Heath

Holly

H olly always wins games
O lly is Ben's third friend
L ions are my second best animal
L ions roar and I like it
Y ellow is George's best colour.

Holly French (6)
Bushey Heath Primary School, Bushey Heath

Poppy

P onies and horses I love the best
O ranges are juicy fruits
P onies are my favourite toys
P oppies are my favourite flowers
Y oghurts are yuck!

Poppy Ainslie (7)
Bushey Heath Primary School, Bushey Heath

My First Acrostic - The South

Ethan

E lectric guitars are my favourite instrument
T horpe Park is my favourite place
H amleys is a big toy shop
A drink is what I like to taste
N o homework is not very good.

Ethan Bradley (6)
Bushey Heath Primary School, Bushey Heath

Jack

J elly is my favourite food
A chocolate chip cookie is yummy
C andyfloss is sugary
K icking a football is fun.

Jack James (6)
Bushey Heath Primary School, Bushey Heath

Anna

A pples are my favourite
N uts are my worst
N anna is the best
A ntennae are scary.

Anna Finley (6)
Bushey Heath Primary School, Bushey Heath

Ben

B eing lazy I really like
E ven TV I watch the most
N ow I'm turning seven.

Ben Fullman (7)
Bushey Heath Primary School, Bushey Heath

Mya O'Grady

M y brother loves me
Y ellow is my favourite colour
A ll people help me

O n Tuesdays I go dancing
G orilla is what I am
R un when I get scared
A picnic on the bench is what I have on Saturdays
D ad loves me lots
Y ummy! Chocolate ice cream.

Mya O'Grady (7)
Castle Hill Infant School, Basingstoke

Isabel

I n the morning I like to watch TV
S aturday I am not at school
A nd when I am at school I read and write
B ut I like to draw
E very day I like my teachers
L ollipops I eat.

Isabel Tarry (6)
Castle Hill Infant School, Basingstoke

My First Acrostic – The South

My Poem

K atherine likes her sister Alexandra
A kitten is my favourite pet
T iger is my second favourite animal
H annah is my friend
E ggs are nice to eat
R eally healthy too
I 've seen a rainbow
N umeracy is very fun
E nglish can be great fun learning to write poems.

Katherine Monk (6)
Castle Hill Infant School, Basingstoke

Silly Keeleigh

K angaroo Keeleigh loves to dance
E very time she goes to the shine glitter disco
E veryone loves bouncy kangaroo Keeleigh
L oves kangaroo mum and gorilla dad
E veryone makes me smile
I love to sing and groove
G iggle Keeleigh's hair is beautiful and soft
H ides when we play hide-and-seek.

Keeleigh Vint (6)
Castle Hill Infant School, Basingstoke

Jessica

- J elly Jessica likes to wibble wobble
- E ven I like to do the jelly welly dance
- S crambled eggs are my favourite egg
- S ometimes I play with my Polly Pocket
- I like hockey
- C armen is my best friend
- A nts are the best bug.

Jessica Gillman (6)
Castle Hill Infant School, Basingstoke

Parnika

- P eople play with me
- A ll people help me when I get hurt
- R eally trying hard at maths
- N ever naughty in school
- I like chocolate ice cream yum-yum!
- K ittens I love so soft and fluffy
- A lways like to go to discos.

Parnika Agrawal (6)
Castle Hill Infant School, Basingstoke

All About Me

- E very day I wake up and eat my breakfast
- R un to school with my mum and my sister
- I like to learn with group Michaelangelo and my friends
- N early everyone in my class is one of my friends.

Erin Riggall (6)
Castle Hill Infant School, Basingstoke

My First Acrostic - The South

Friend

S hannon is always laughing
H appy Shannon is lovely
A ll my friends think I'm clever
N early everyone loves me
N ever naughty
O ne of my friends
N one of my friends think I'm naughty.

Shannon Crawford (6)
Castle Hill Infant School, Basingstoke

Rebecca

R ebecca is good
E ver so good at dancing
B etter at swimming
E ats cakes
C an you help me?
C an you help?
A nts are horrible.

Rebecca Dark (6)
Castle Hill Infant School, Basingstoke

Toby

T rouble, Toby always makes trouble
O h no I have bigger feet than my sister
B acon in sandwiches with ketchup is lovely
Y ummy I love yoghurt, mmmmm.

Toby Micallef (6)
Castle Hill Infant School, Basingstoke

Charlie's Life

C harlie likes playing New Super Mario Brothers
H ates salad
A shley Young is a loser
R ooney is awesome
L ikes Ronaldo
I like Club Penguin
E mpty bins is a job for me.

Charlie Pergusey (7)
Castle Hill Infant School, Basingstoke

All About William

W ill likes Steven Gerrard
I n his brain he talks a lot
L ike a chatty box
L emonade is his favourite drink
I nterested in football
A fan of monkeys
M akes a lot of cakes at home.

William Browne (7)
Castle Hill Infant School, Basingstoke

Lovely Ella

E lla is always happy
L ovely to laugh and giggle
L ovely Ella likes to play
A lways playing with my kind friends.

Ella Bennett (6)
Castle Hill Infant School, Basingstoke

My First Acrostic - The South

Bradley

B radley is a cheeky monkey
R unning from the start
A pples are juicy
D ad is fun
L and the plane when I play
E ggs are delicious
Y ay! I win.

Bradley Clarke (7)
Castle Hill Infant School, Basingstoke

Hannah

H annah is my name and I like playing
A friend is a best friend
N umbers go on forever
N eptune is a planet and it is interesting
A lready so happy
H elpful Hannah always helping.

Hannah Chamberlain (6)
Castle Hill Infant School, Basingstoke

About Me

L ibby is my name
I like sleepovers when people come over
B alls are my thing
B ecky is my friend
Y o-yos are my favourite.

Libby Bonner (7)
Castle Hill Infant School, Basingstoke

Smiley Abitha

A cting is my favourite thing
B adgers are great for me
I ce Age is the best
T o Abitha, you can come to my birthday!
'H ola Miss Cordery,' I say. Other people say that as well.
A rt is my favourite.

Abitha Nanthakumar (6)
Castle Hill Infant School, Basingstoke

Joshua

J oshua is my name
O h I went to my dad's
S illy sentences I write
H appy I am
U nder my bed I hide things
A pples are my favourite fruit.

Joshua Challis (6)
Castle Hill Infant School, Basingstoke

Sophie

S ophie is my best friend
O ften being funny
P retending to be a cat
H elping each other
I n the playground she plays with me
E very day in the playground I play with Shannon.

Sophie Murray-Cousens (7)
Castle Hill Infant School, Basingstoke

My First Acrostic - The South

Connor

C onnor plays games on the playground
O n Tuesday he goes to swimming lessons
N o I don't go home after school
N ice I am
O n Monday I go to school
R oses are my favourite.

Connor Richardson (6)
Castle Hill Infant School, Basingstoke

Harley

H arley is better than Will at football
A pples are juicy and Harley loves them
R ooney is better than Harley
L emonade is my favourite drink
E lephants are not pets
Y ou are reading my poem.

Harley Bateman (6)
Castle Hill Infant School, Basingstoke

Simran

S miley and kind but a bit grumpy
I love my friends at school
M arvellous me, also fabulous sister when she is there for me
R ight in maths, sometimes bad in English
A lways so happy I'm home with Mummy and daddy
N ow and then a little shy I am.

Simran Atwal (6)
Castle Hill Infant School, Basingstoke

Kind Hannah

H appy Hannah is always happy
A nd good at PE
N o one is as good at smiles as me
N uggets are delicious
A lways I play with my friends
H ope Hannah likes shopping.

Hannah Rogers-Mitchell (6)
Castle Hill Infant School, Basingstoke

Kieran

K ieran is funny
I 'm good at football
E verybody is my friend
R iding on my bike is funny
A fter school I go to afterschool club
N obody is not my friend.

Kieran Davidson-Blake (6)
Castle Hill Infant School, Basingstoke

My Life

J okes I make are funny
O ranges are tasty
S am is my brother
H arry is my friend
U seful is me
A rgentina losers!

Joshua Allen (6)
Castle Hill Infant School, Basingstoke

My First Acrostic - The South

Connor

C ould be five or six
O h no I fall over sometimes
N ice teacher I have
N o you can't have yummy cookies
O range juice is my favourite
R eally soft brown hair.

Connor Solley-Andrews (6)
Castle Hill Infant School, Basingstoke

Milly

M illy is beautiful
I love pink
L unch is my favourite time of the day
L ittle little brother
Y oghurts are my favourite.

Milly Toombes (6)
Castle Hill Infant School, Basingstoke

Lexie

L exie running to school
E veryone laughs at me
eX tra kind
I like my friends
E veryone likes me.

Lexie King (6)
Castle Hill Infant School, Basingstoke

Cool Poem

M ason is good at football
A nd cool in the playground
S o cool I share
O n and off the pitch I play football
N ow I will play with Harry.

Mason Knott (6)
Castle Hill Infant School, Basingstoke

Good James

J elly belly James
A ll my friends say I am happy
M y daddy makes me happy
E nergy, I have lots when I run
S ee my sparkling brown eyes.

James Lyness (7)
Castle Hill Infant School, Basingstoke

Smiley Aryun

A rt is my favourite thing
R eally nice when I am with Conner
Y ummy, yummy, in my tummy, chocolate I love
U nfair - I want some sweets
N aughty brother, give me that!

Aryun Banga (6)
Castle Hill Infant School, Basingstoke

My First Acrostic - The South

Harry

H ello my name is Harry
A nd I'm cool in the playground
R oy is my favourite programme
R ooney is who I support
Y o-yos are fun.

Harry Wells (6)
Castle Hill Infant School, Basingstoke

Craig

C oco Craig likes coconuts
R oar! I like tigers
A pes are cheeky like me
I 'm animal mad
G etting happy again.

Craig Stock (6)
Castle Hill Infant School, Basingstoke

Lewis

L ewis is my name and I like playing football
E very day I play with funny friends
W onderful words I have in my head
I like playing with my friends especially when I go round to their house
S miley but a bit angry!

Lewis Hall (7)
Castle Hill Infant School, Basingstoke

Renee

R enee is my name
E very day I eat sandwiches
N obody plays in my form
E llie is my friend
E aster is my favourite time.

Renee Mhuri (6)
Castle Hill Infant School, Basingstoke

Ryan

R yan helped Riley
Y esterday
A nd Riley helped me
N ice to Mummy too.

Ryan Lock (6)
Castle Hill Infant School, Basingstoke

Dinosaurs

D estroying dinosaurs rampaging through the jungle
I nteresting pteradactyl
N oisy dinosaurs roaring
O ften hungry
S cary dinosaurs
A lways stomping
U gly teeth
R oars
S harp teeth biting other dinosaurs.

Max Carvalho (6)
Chilworth CE Aided Infant School, Chilworth

My First Acrostic - The South

Penguins

P enguins eat fish
E xcited always because they get babies
N ever eat humans
G rumpy sometimes
U usually penguins are black and white
I ce is warm for the penguins
N aughty penguins catch very good fish
S outh Pole is where penguins live.

James Jenkins (6)
Chilworth CE Aided Infant School, Chilworth

Hamster

H amsters are cute and fluffy
A nd quick hamsters
M arvellous cages
S pecial white hamsters
T eeth are pointy
E very hamster is brainy
R unning around in the ball
S pecial brown hamster.

Ewa Borzecka (7)
Chilworth CE Aided Infant School, Chilworth

Hamsters

H appy and cute
A pples she likes
M akes me happy when I'm sad
S he sniffs my hand when I put it by the cage
T asty crunching carrots
E very day I fill up her water bottle
R unning around in her silver ball
S he likes tasty food and chocolate drops.

Daisy Dunne (6)
Chilworth CE Aided Infant School, Chilworth

Insects

I nteresting insects
N ice insects
S pider with googly eyes
E xcellent creatures
C limbing caterpillars
T arantulas crawling across the floor
S haped creatures are different.

Joshua Ingham (6)
Chilworth CE Aided Infant School, Chilworth

My First Acrostic - The South

Puppies

P uppies are cute
U nusual colour
P up is my dog
P up's favourite food is crunchy biscuits and bones
I t is sweet!
E xciting, keep him!
S ay 'Woof' in a minute pup.

Sian Gillingham (6)
Chilworth CE Aided Infant School, Chilworth

Puppies

P uppies are cute and very fluffy
U nhappy times
P uppies are gentle all the time
P uppies are glamorous
I nterested in bones
E verywhere good all the time
S oft on the ears.

Connie Sharp (6)
Chilworth CE Aided Infant School, Chilworth

Dogs

D ogs are great because they are cute
O utside they like to run around
G lamorous because they are behaved
S oft because they look great fun and lovely.

Rosie Savage (6)
Chilworth CE Aided Infant School, Chilworth

History

H enry the VIII was a very cruel king
I nteresting to me
S oldiers were killed in the wars
T udors lived a long time ago
O nce in the year it is Guy Fawkes night
R omans fight a lot
Y ikes the Vikings are coming.

Toby Brewer (6)
Chilworth CE Aided Infant School, Chilworth

Dresses

D ancing dresses are pink
R oses are the colour I love
E xcellent dresses look cool
S parkly and silky, soft and smooth
S waying dresses are soft
E legant dresses are beautiful and glamorous
S corching wedding dresses.

Jemma Ellis (6)
Chilworth CE Aided Infant School, Chilworth

Army

A ttack
R un
M achine gun
Y elling.

George Summerfield-Scott (6)
Chilworth CE Aided Infant School, Chilworth

My First Acrostic – The South

Spooky

S harp claws scratch you
P aws very rough
O ften good
O nce he almost caught a mouse
K ittens are cute
Y esterday I cuddled him.

Amelie Butler (6)
Chilworth CE Aided Infant School, Chilworth

Pizza

P epperoni
I love it
Z oom on a bike
Z ap it's here
A ll gone.

James Kinton (6)
Chilworth CE Aided Infant School, Chilworth

Seaside

S uncream
E xciting
A n ice cream
S ea is deep
I ce cream
D anger!
E veryone is having fun.

Harry Duffy (6)
Edward Betham CE Primary School, Greenford

Seaside Rescue

S and is soft and warm
E xcited children play catch
A big wave splashed me
S omeone was in the water
I played in the sand
D ripping in the water
E veryone is in the water

R escue the people
E agles are on the sand
S ome people were hot
C all the people to help
U se some suncream
E agles were at the seaside.

Laura Eshun (6)
Edward Betham CE Primary School, Greenford

Seaside

S and all around my feet
E agles flying above my head
A ngry men shouting at each other
S *plish splash* I hear water
I nside the rock I saw a starfish
D ive quickly
E veryone is having fun in the water.

David Morohunfola (7)
Edward Betham CE Primary School, Greenford

My First Acrostic - The South

Seaside Rescue

S and so soft, oh so soft and runny
E veryone have fun in the water
A ll of the people are having fun
S o you join in as well
I like this tasty ice cream, *yum yum*
D o the coconut dance everyone
E ach and everyone of us is partying

R ough boys playing beach ball
E agles flapping madly
S unny sun is shining on us
C ute dogs are laying down
U se your buckets and spades everyone
E veryone will go home soon.

Cerys McNeil (7)
Edward Betham CE Primary School, Greenford

Shell

S mooth
H arbour
E legant
L arge
L uminous.

Jhokasta Candelas (6)
Edward Betham CE Primary School, Greenford

Seaside Rescue

S and in between my toes
E verybody is in the water
A man is selling doughnuts
S ee me swim
I am making a sandcastle
D ive in the water
E verybody help me

R un in the water
E ager people rescue
S omeone come, Dad is drowning!
C an you help me rescue him?
U se the lifeboat
E veryone is safe.

Isabel Hunte-Wood (6)
Edward Betham CE Primary School, Greenford

Beach

B each
E veryone
A the beach is
C alm and
H ot.

Joshua Grant-McKenzie (7)
Edward Betham CE Primary School, Greenford

My First Acrostic - The South

Seaside Rescue

S un is shining while I'm in the water
E agles squawking in the sky
A person is in danger
S and is far from the boy
I phoned the coastguard quickly
D anger is flowing
E ager children wanting to play with the boy

R eady to launch
E veryone's here
S et it up to go in the sea
C oming quick
U se the rope
E nd of the rescue.

Mia Thomas (7)
Edward Betham CE Primary School, Greenford

Shells

S mooth shells
H eavy shells
E xcellent shells
L isten to the sea
L ovely rough shells.

Hailey Sathyavan (6)
Edward Betham CE Primary School, Greenford

Seaside Rescue

S *plish splash,* I'm swimming in the sea
E agles flying in the sky
A fish swimming in the sea
S un flashing on me
I buried myself in the sand
D ig, dig in the sand
E veryone wants to swim in the sea

R escue guards come and save us
E veryone rescues the person in trouble
S omeone is in trouble
C ome as fast as you can
U mbrella making the sun not go on me
E verything is safe and sound.

Hazel Sathyavan (6)
Edward Betham CE Primary School, Greenford

Shell

S hells are on the beach
H uts for people changing
E veryone having fun
L ighthouse shining
L ots of people sunbathing.

Semra Karakaya (6)
Edward Betham CE Primary School, Greenford

My First Acrostic - The South

Seaside Rescue

S and was going in the pool
E veryone was splashing in the water
A big wave was coming
S *plash* went the water
I saw the water coming towards the sand
D ig the sand
E veryone was lying on the water

R escue him, he is drowning
E veryone was in the water
S omeone was under the water
C ome on let's rescue him
U nder the water I saw a shadow
E agles were on the sand.

Adrine Andreasian (6)
Edward Betham CE Primary School, Greenford

Shell

S hiny
H ard
E legant
L uscious
L onely.

Sophia Tebbit (6)
Edward Betham CE Primary School, Greenford

Seaside Rescue

S and so tickly
E xcited people playing
A man was playing with a ball
S and between my toes
I went home
D ig, dig, dig!
E at your ice cream

R un
E veryone's in trouble
S ail the lifeboat
C old water
U se a shovel to dig
E veryone went home.

Robbie Blair (6)
Edward Betham CE Primary School, Greenford

Beach

B each ball
E njoyment
A n ice cream for everyone
C hildren have fun
H arbour for the boat.

David Akinwande (7)
Edward Betham CE Primary School, Greenford

My First Acrostic - The South

Seaside Rescue

S ea is wavy
E agles squawking excitedly
A boy is in trouble
S easide rescue get a call
I watched the boat
D own the rescue centre they launched the boat
E mergency, the next boy was in trouble

R escue centre gets another call
E agle calls the coastguard
S ea was wavy
C ome and see a sandcastle
U se my bucket and spade to play with my friends
E verybody got wet.

Frankie Snell (6)
Edward Betham CE Primary School, Greenford

Water Rescue

W ater splashing, someone is in trouble
A s the underwater crew came to help
T o save anyone who's in trouble underwater
E mbark on the journey
R ace under the water

R escue the person under the deep sea
E ngine down, oh no! We need more oil!
S omeone's there, it's a swimmer. Hello!
C unning fish swimming in the sea
U nder there, what is it? It's the person
E veryone is safe and the expedition is finished!

Kyza Tettey (6)
Edward Betham CE Primary School, Greenford

Water Rescue

W eather is bad
A boat is sinking
T oes are in the water
E veryone is watching
R escue the boat

R eady to go?
E veryone is scared
S tay calm
C ome to save me!
U gent! Urgent!
E veryone is happy.

Jack O'Gara (6)
Edward Betham CE Primary School, Greenford

My First Acrostic - The South

Water Rescue

W ater is crashing
A ship is sinking, help everyone
T ell the lifeguard
E mergency! Emergency!
R escue everyone! Rescue everyone!

R eady to go down the slope
E xcellent!
S ave all the people on the ship
C linging onto the rocks is what they are doing
U se a boat to rescue them
E veryone is safe.

Lydia Malecaut (6)
Edward Betham CE Primary School, Greenford

Water Rescue

W hat is that noise?
A little boy is in trouble
T oes in the sea
E veryone is happy
R escue the little boy someone

R escue him quick
E veryone is scared. The little boy might drown
S omeone rescue him
C rashing waves
U rgent!
E veryone is safe.

Pierre Metry (7)
Edward Betham CE Primary School, Greenford

Water Rescue

W e need to go and save
A boy who is drowning in
T he Atlantic Ocean and we need to
E mbark on our mission to
R escue him

R ing the fire alarm and are you ready?
E xcellent!
S aving a boy is fun
C ome on
U ntil the
E xpedition is finished.

Dante George (6)
Edward Betham CE Primary School, Greenford

Water Rescue

W arning
A girl is
T urning the wrong way
E xciting
R eady to go?

R ed flag is emergency
E veryone is shouting
S ea
C ool sea
U nderwater the girl is safe
E mergency over.

Adam Hayward (6)
Edward Betham CE Primary School, Greenford

My First Acrostic - The South

Florence Nightingale

F lorence is a nurse
L ikes to be a nurse
O ranges are her favourite fruit
R ushing everywhere
E very hospital is dirty she makes it
N ice and clean
C lean and clumsy everywhere
E veryone likes her

N urse Florence
I n Scutari Hospital
G oing to help the soldiers
H elpful and kind
T erribly nice
I n the hospital
N ice to everyone
G oes Florence
A ll around the hospital
L ovely and kind
E very day.

Frederick Falk (6)
Farleigh School, Andover

Lara

L ovely Lara is six
A nxious sometimes
R eally ready to work
A lways really nice

S ometimes silly
M essy at lunch
I n the lunch hall
T hinks things are tasty
H olly is her best friend

O K in school
S ometimes a silly sausage
B ehaves well
O K at her work
U sually good
R eady to rock
N ever upset
E xtremely good at making things.

Lara Smyth-Osbourne (6)
Farleigh School, Andover

Angus

A uthor
N ice
G reat
U pset
S miley.

Angus Mihell (6)
Farleigh School, Andover

My First Acrostic - The South

James

J ames is seven
A mazing at football
M akes lots of friends
E njoys scoring lots of goals
S ometimes lets goals in

R eally likes cricket
O vers are quick
B owls straight
E xtremely better than Ricky Ponting
R eally makes effort
T ries to get him out

H ungry as a pig
A lways eats meat
Y um-yum in my tum
E xtremely fat
S ometimes is messy.

James Hayes (7)
Farleigh School, Andover

Edward

E d is excited
D rinks tea
W onderful at spellings
A lways good at making things
R uns fast
D oes sewing.

Ed Betton (6)
Farleigh School, Andover

Holly

H olly is seven and very happy
O ranges are her favourite
L ara is her best friend
L ovely and kind
Y oghurt is her favourite

B illy is her friend
E ats eggs a lot
N ice and kind
T icklish and funny
L ikes giraffes a lot
E gypt is her favourite place
Y ummy as a lolly.

Holly Bentley (7)
Farleigh School, Andover

Horses

T ractors are fun
H orses are great
O ld ponies are steady
R earranging jumps
N ext I win the bending race
H orses' houses are called stables
I n the stables horses are munching hay
L ove horses they are the best
L ovely ponies they are brilliant.

Saffron Davie-Thornhill (6)
Farleigh School, Andover

My First Acrostic - The South

Millie

M illie is miserable
I s extremely good at making things
L ovely work Millie does
L ovely hair she has
I s extremely nice
E asy to spell

U nbelievably kind
R eally breezy
S hy but nice
E xpects questions
L ovely manners
L ikes lollies.

Amelia Ursell (6)
Farleigh School, Andover

Sebastian

S ebastian is silly
E xtremely afraid of ghosts
B ehaviour is appalling
A ttitude is bad
S hy and selfish
T alking too much
I n the classroom
A fraid of everything
N ice to his friends.

Sebastian Kilpatrick (6)
Farleigh School, Andover

Florence Nightingale

F lorence was a nurse
L ovely to the soldiers
O ctober she was born
R eally likes cleaning
E ven the toilets
N ice to everyone
C hanged the hospitals
E veryone liked her.

Amelie Osborn-Smith (6)
Farleigh School, Andover

Charlie

C harlie
H appy
A uthor
R acing
L ovely
I gloo
E xcited.

Charlie MacDonald-Smith (6)
Farleigh School, Andover

My First Acrostic - The South

Thomas

T om is best
H e beats everyone else
O n the other team
M akes it to the finals
A nd wins the trophy
S urprised himself.

Thomas Harvie-Watt (6)
Farleigh School, Andover

Horrid Henry

H orrid to people
E xtremely bad
N aughty to people
R ubbish
Y ou stink.

William Marsh (6)
Farleigh School, Andover

My Friend

R eally nice
A nxious
L ucky
P erfect
H elpful.

Béla Jankovich Besan (6)
Farleigh School, Andover

Michael's Beautiful Poem

M ad when somebody is mean
I am good at football
C an do lovely handwriting
H elping people
A really good person
E xcellent at numbers up to 1000
L oud sometimes

C an get lots of team points
R acing on my PlayStation
I love to write
L iking this class
L ove to go to bed
E ating lots of food
Y es I've got friends.

Michael Crilley (6)
Foxmoor School, Stroud

All About Me

B rave when I fall over
E xcited at everything
N aughty outside

B eautiful Ben
R ough Ben
O ptimistic Ben
W icked Ben
N oisy Ben.

Ben Brown (6)
Foxmoor School, Stroud

My First Acrostic - The South

A Beautiful Bryony Poem

B eautiful every day
R unning safely on the path
Y o-yo's are fun
O utside is fun
N o one annoys me
Y oung is good

B ikes are good to play on
U K is a world that is the best
C atching a ball is my favourite
K ill is not a very nice word
L ollies are nice to eat
A pples are the best
N avy is a good colour
D ogs are stinky.

Bryony Buckland (6)
Foxmoor School, Stroud

Phonetic Phoenix

P retty Phoenix
H appy to play with her friends
O ranges are her favourite snack
E very day she is smart
N ever naughty
I n school she works hard
X tremely kind.

Phoenix Dangerfield (6)
Foxmoor School, Stroud

All About Me

C ute me
H appy with my friends
A really good friend all the time
R eady for work at school
L ikeable for friends
I am good at art
E xcellent me

P icking flowers at school
E xcited
A cting with my two friends
R acket at my home
C aring all the time
E nergetic.

Charlie Pearce (7)
Foxmoor School, Stroud

All About Me

M arvellous and nice
A ctive and stretchy
I ntelligent and focused
S illy and crazy
E nergetic and hyper
Y ellowy blondey hair.

Maisey Hammond (6)
Foxmoor School, Stroud

My First Acrostic – The South

A Wonder About Me

Z oomy at reading
A ctive in the morning
C rackers in the afternoon
K ind in the night

E xcellent at football
C razy after school
K ind boy
E nergetic at running
R ubbish at rugby
S illy and funny
A crobatic
L ong football shot
L oopy as a hulahoop.

Zack Eckersall (6)
Foxmoor School, Stroud

Fabulous Tia

T errible
I am special
A ctive in the morning
R usty in the afternoon
N oisy at home
A cting is cool.

Tiarna Crowther (6)
Foxmoor School, Stroud

Trouble Tom

T rouble to my brother
O ptimistic I am
M ucky I am

P roud of everything
I 'm nice
C ool at school
K ind to everybody
E xcellent at football
R ough outside, good inside
I 'm delicate, well sort of!
N oisy I am
G ood to everyone.

Tom Pickering (6)
Foxmoor School, Stroud

I'm Ellis

E xcellent at football
L ovely Ellis
L ikeable Ellis
I like chocolate
S low bike riding

H appy at the computer
E veryone is friendly
A ngry Ellis
T ricky at drawing
H elpful to everyone.

Ellis Heath (6)
Foxmoor School, Stroud

My First Acrostic - The South

My Life

I run all the time
W ealthy
A ctive person
N ice person

R acing a lot
O ptimisitic
S ecretive
S inging twice a month
I like science
T all but not very
E at night and day
R eally, really fast.

Iwan Rossiter (6)
Foxmoor School, Stroud

Beth Wow Wow

B eautiful Beth
E xcellent I am
T idy that's me
H elpful to everybody

F unny oh yes
O h I am happy
W onderful at art
L oud, when playing
E xcited me
S illy and fun.

Beth Fowles (6)
Foxmoor School, Stroud

All About Me

M arvellous at keeping tidy
I ntelligent
A ngry when Kieran annoys me

G iggly at playtime
A ctive
R ough
D addy likes me
E nergetic
N aughty
E ach day I am really good
R eally good friend.

Mia Gardener (6)
Foxmoor School, Stroud

All About Me

A ngel in the sky
L ovely Alice
I am beautiful
C uddly and friendly
E nergetic at running.

Alice Hill (6)
Foxmoor School, Stroud

My First Acrostic - The South

Dinosaurs Everywhere

D on't go near them
I n your garden
N aughty mean dinosaurs
O ver there is a pteradactyl
S tanding in the sky
A nd falling from the air
U nder my bed I saw a velociraptor
R unning to the start line
S tegosaurus and triceratops racing.

Alex Bennett (6)
Harlyn Primary School, Pinner

Holidays

H appy times with my family
O n the beach
L ucy loves being in the sea
I n the icy cold water
D addy wraps me in a towel
A nd cuddles me to get warm
Y ummy ice lollies
S and in my toes which feels tickly.

Lucy Sutch (6)
Harlyn Primary School, Pinner

Puppies

P uppies are naughty
U p to some trouble
P laying around with their favourite toy
P uppies are cute
I love them so much
E verything they do is
S o adorable.

Sophia Kerridge (6)
Harlyn Primary School, Pinner

Flowers

F lowers are beautiful. I love their smell
L eaves and stems are nice and green
O rchids are my favourite flower
W eeds are not welcome
E veryone should have a flower
R ed roses look good in vases
S unflowers are bright. They make everyone smile.

Amba Mehta (5)
Harlyn Primary School, Pinner

My First Acrostic - The South

Big Sun

B ig Sun, Big Sun, how are you?
I n the sky, how do you do?
G reat Big Sun, do you want to play?

S un so big, it's up to you.
U p in the sky, you can decide.
N ow we can play all day outside.

Ethan Crockford (6)
Harlyn Primary School, Pinner

Autumn

A utumn is when the leaves fall down
U nder the trees all golden brown
T here's no need for a hat on my head
U p in the sky the sun's now in bed
M ornings the sky is clear
N ow that winter is nearly here.

Eloise Curtis (5)
Harlyn Primary School, Pinner

Me

S ophie is my name
O ctober is when I was born
P laying with my friends is what I do the most
H aving two brothers is so much fun
I love High School Musical
E very day is so much fun.

Sophie Jenkins (6)
Harlyn Primary School, Pinner

Apple

A n apple is sweet

P ick some apples with me

P eel some apples with me

L ovely apples in a pie

E veryone have a slice.

Emily Barnard (6)
Harlyn Primary School, Pinner

Sport

S port is very healthy

P laying games is fun

O nly when you win you are number one

R unning, skipping and jumping is good for your heart

T rying your best to do your part.

Ashwin Sangarpaul (5)
Harlyn Primary School, Pinner

Teddy

T idy up teddy

E at some food

D o your brushy

D on't make a mess

Y ou are my friend.

Jasmine Tailor (6)
Harlyn Primary School, Pinner

My First Acrostic - The South

Brother

B rave as a lion
R uns really fast
O ften crazy
T otally fun
H as a toy car
E ats quickly
R eally good fun.

Blake Penwarden (6)
Holy Apostles CE Primary School, Cheltenham

Grandpa

G randpa is great
R eally kind
A lways adventurous
N ice always
D addy loves him
P lays with me
A nd I love him too.

Jack Wilkins (6)
Holy Apostles CE Primary School, Cheltenham

Grandad

G reat at cheering
R eally noisy
A big man
N aughty sometimes
D rinks lots of beer
A big fan of Man United
D rives a silver car.

Jacob Adams (7)
Holy Apostles CE Primary School, Cheltenham

Mummy

M ummy likes to cook
U ses the computer
M ummy always cleans up
M ummy eats peas and carrots
Y ou are a clever mum.

Faneem Mansoon (6)
Holy Apostles CE Primary School, Cheltenham

Daddy

D ad is very funny
A nd he drinks beer
D oes a lot of building work
D aring me to be funny
Y oung at forty.

Leo Daubeney (6)
Holy Apostles CE Primary School, Cheltenham

My First Acrostic - The South

Daddy

D ad plays the organ
A lways kind to me
D oesn't shout too much
D ad is sometimes cheeky
Y ou are forty five!

Sophie Cole (6)
Holy Apostles CE Primary School, Cheltenham

Mummy

M ummy does silly voices to make me laugh
U ses a bike to take me to school
M akes delicious spaghetti Bolognese
M akes me feel proud because she did the triathalon
Y ou are the best mummy in the whole world.

Sam Seeley (6)
Holy Apostles CE Primary School, Cheltenham

Cameron

C ameron is crazy
A m a good boy
M e, I am good
E at, I can eat
R eading, I am reading
O h I am playing by myself
N ice, I am nice.

Cameron Carlton (7)
Holy Family RC Primary School, London

Miss Conway

M y teacher is bonkers
I like my teacher
S trict Miss Conway
S illy teacher

C ute Miss Conway
O nly teacher
N ice woman
W e like Miss Conway
A very nice teacher
Y ou're nice.

Maisie Sykes (7)
Holy Family RC Primary School, London

John Sawyer

J acob is my friend
O ctopuses are my favourite animal
H annah Montana is not my favourite
N ow I like computer games

S ounds are my favourite
A saria is my special friend
W hales are friendly
Y oghurt is my favourite
E dward is my favourite
R E is not really my favourite.

John Sawyer (6)
Holy Family RC Primary School, London

My First Acrostic - The South

William

W illiam loves playing football
I n my home I love playing on the DS
L isten to my mum
L ive in my home
I love a book
A concert is colourful
M y snowman has melted.

William Li (7)
Holy Family RC Primary School, London

Daniel

D aniel is from Vietnam
A nd crazy, bonkers
N ame me, I am Daniel
I am Daniel
E at your beans, I do
L ick your lollipop.

Daniel Li Nguyen (5)
Holy Family RC Primary School, London

Grace

G race is a star
R ainbows are beautiful like me
A nimals are my favourite
C ute Grace is funny
E lephants are my favourite.

Grace Beautyman (6)
Holy Family RC Primary School, London

Serena

S erena is a superstar!
E llie is my best friend!
R enee is crazy!
E llie is beautiful!
N guyen is nice!
A lana is brilliant!

Serena Hapurachilagai (7)
Holy Family RC Primary School, London

Ermias

E rmias is a superstar
R oses are blue
M y friend plays football
I play football
A ll my friends play with me
S inging is fun.

Ermias Wondwossen Hailu (7)
Holy Family RC Primary School, London

Friend

F riendly
R espect
I ndependent
E asy
N ice
D elightful.

Azaria Kidane (6)
Holy Family RC Primary School, London

My First Acrostic - The South

Roses

R oses are pretty!
O pen up, my beautiful roses!
S pring is coming, so open up my beautiful roses!
E xciting things will happen, so open up!
S pring is going, so please open up my beautiful roses.

Leah Ellie Wren (6)
Holy Family RC Primary School, London

Roses

R oses are beautiful
O pen the beautiful roses
S pring is coming, so open up roses
E xciting roses please come out
S pring is coming, so please come out.

Lashae Julius (6)
Holy Family RC Primary School, London

Rugby

R ugby is a hard game
U se a rugby ball
G rumpy games
B arking Club
Y ou are a great rugby team.

Joseph Davies (7)
Holy Family RC Primary School, London

Megan

M egan is lazy, crazy!
E mily is my funny friend!
G great food
A pple is my favourite fruit
N ice cats.

Megan Rafat (6)
Holy Family RC Primary School, London

Demi

D emi is clever
E llie is beautiful
M y best friend is Leah
I love my mum and dad.

Demi Mifsud (6)
Holy Family RC Primary School, London

Star

S tars are light
T he stars are beautiful
A star is like an apple
R espect the stars.

Ronnie Heavey (6)
Holy Family RC Primary School, London

My First Acrostic - The South

Bolu

B olu is from Nigeria
O h la la
L uke
U are nice.

Bolu Shobowale (6)
Holy Family RC Primary School, London

Mum

M y mum treats me like a star
U are the best mum
M y mum is a star.

Renee Palmer (6)
Holy Family RC Primary School, London

The Seaside

S easides are sunny
E ating ice cream is yummy
A speedboat whizzing around in the sea
S eagulls fly in the air
I saw a fairground on the pier
D olphins diving in the sea
E ating a picnic on the beach.

Rosie Farney (6)
Lime Walk Primary School, Hemel Hempstead

The Seaside

S eagulls do a funny squawk
E veryday the sun is out
A rcades are fun!
S peedboats go fast
I ce cream is cold
D olphins jump out of the sea
E ating a crab for my tea!

Tobi Pocock (6)
Lime Walk Primary School, Hemel Hempstead

The Seaside

S oft, yellow sand is fun to play in
E ating a picnic behind a sand dune
A rcades are fun to go to
S peedboats go very fast
I ce cream is yummy
D ad's sunbathing
E ating cake is yummy!

Kai Gordon (6)
Lime Walk Primary School, Hemel Hempstead

Myself!

J umps
A lways plays basketball
K icks a football
E veryday I go to school it's fun!

Jake Final (6)
Lime Walk Primary School, Hemel Hempstead

My First Acrostic - The South

The Seaside

S ea is fun and you can swim in it
E veryday it is sunny
A n ice cream man came
S eagulls squawking
I can swim in the sea
D o a sandcastle
E ating food.

Josh King (6)
Lime Walk Primary School, Hemel Hempstead

The Seaside

S andy beach is the best ever
E veryday I build sandcastles
A seagull swooped down and grabbed a fish
S ome people go fishing there
I love eating candyfloss on the beach
D ad is eating ice cream
E very day the sun shines.

Hannah Nicholson (6)
Lime Walk Primary School, Hemel Hempstead

The Seaside

S and
E ating crab
A seagull squeaking
S ea nice and warm
I love ice cream!
D ad laying on the sand
E very day I go in my boat.

Luke Thomas (6)
Lime Walk Primary School, Hemel Hempstead

The Seaside

S and is fun to play in
E at fish and chips
A rcades are fun to play in
S eagulls squawking
I can see a lighthouse
D o massive sandcastles!
E very day the sun is shining.

Thomas Borrowdale (6)
Lime Walk Primary School, Hemel Hempstead

My First Acrostic - The South

Myself!

M ehrin is happy!
E veryday she goes to school
H er brother is silly
R osie is her best friend
I n her room there are red walls
N ever scared of spiders!

Mehrin Ahmed (6)
Lime Walk Primary School, Hemel Hempstead

Myself!

L uke is cool!
U ses good words in his work
K ind to his friends
E asily does sums

J ack is my best friend.

Luke Jenkins (6)
Lime Walk Primary School, Hemel Hempstead

Myself!

K azie is kind today
A pples are good for you
Z alikha is my friend
I like to play football
E xcited for Christmas!

Kazie Dufaur-Green (6)
Lime Walk Primary School, Hemel Hempstead

Planets

P lanets glide gracefully in the pitch-black darkness of space
L ovely and secret things to be explored
A ll the stars glimmer and flash around the Earth
And the moon shines
N ice planets have baby stars, the moon has two
E agle lands on the bumpy moon, astronauts hopped
Around the moon
T he great things in space are special
S parkling magical stars flashing and shooting gracefully.

Sky Cassels (6)
Ramsey Manor Lower School, Barton Le Clay

Planets

P lanets they are round like a ball
L ittle shiny twinkly stars shining at night
A round the Earth the moon goes, around the Earth
The sun goes around the moon
N eil Armstrong was the first man on the moon
E agle was the kind of rocket to land on the moon
T winkly stars above the Earth
S hiny moon, sandy moon.

Ciaran Moore (6)
Ramsey Manor Lower School, Barton Le Clay

My First Acrostic - The South

Planets

P lanets gliding slowly around the darkness
L ight sun beaming like a volcano in the dark
A stronauts take one small step for Man,
   One giant leap for Mankind
N eil Armstrong was the first man to step on the moon
E agle was the first vehicle to land on the moon
T wisting planets everywhere
S aturn's rings are beautiful colours.

Holly Brennan (6)
Ramsey Manor Lower School, Barton Le Clay

Planets

P lanets gliding in the darkness
L ike dizzy planets that are smooth
A stronauts take one small step for Man,
   One giant step for Mankind
N eil Armstrong was the first man to walk on the moon
E agle was the vehicle he used on the moon
T wirling slowly
S aturn rings and glittering planets.

Ella Revels (6)
Ramsey Manor Lower School, Barton Le Clay

Planets

P lanets are very colourful
L ight is busting from the sun
A stronauts go very high up
N eil Armsxtrong and friends were the first men to step on the moon
E agle was Neil's landing rocket
T urning like some planets
S aturn is the best and colourful planet.

Courtney Rogers (6)
Ramsey Manor Lower School, Barton Le Clay

Planets

P lanets zooming in space
L anding on the moon
A pollo took off, the rocket
N eil was the first man on the moon
E normous moon, why are you so big?
T he sights to behold
S cientists discovered that Pluto was a star.

Joseph Edmunds (6)
Ramsey Manor Lower School, Barton Le Clay

My First Acrostic - The South

Planets

P lanets moving around space
L ight from the sun shining bright
A stronauts landing on the moon
N asty sun shooting out fire
E normous world jiggling around
T wirling stars shooting around the moon
S tars jumping around the moon.

Tilly Haestier (6)
Ramsey Manor Lower School, Barton Le Clay

Planets

P lanets twirl around and around
L ight flashing bright from hot sun
A pollo
N eptune spins slowly
E normous planets
T wisting planets get dizzy
S aturn's rings are circles.

Abigail Green (6)
Ramsey Manor Lower School, Barton Le Clay

Planets

P lanets glide carefully around the boiling sun
L oads of planets glide around the universe
A stronauts bounce on the moon
N eptune is so purple
E agle landed on the moon in space
T wisting planets around the moon
S unlight with planets beside.

Kate Kilby (6)
Ramsey Manor Lower School, Barton Le Clay

Planets

P lanets zooming in space
L ittle planets floating
A stronauts floating in space
N eil Armstrong was the first man to step on the moon
E agle was his landing rocket
T winkling stars shining so high
S hining moon, bus on the moon.

Finlay Dolan (6)
Ramsey Manor Lower School, Barton Le Clay

My First Acrostic - The South

Planets

P lanets glide slowly in the darkness
L ittle stars floating like astronauts would in a rocket
A mazing sights up by the rainbow - coloured and twirling planets
N eptune is all purple and blue
E verywhere in the night sky there is always a shiny planet
T iny planets all over the universe
S hining twinkling stars glowing all over the night sky.

Isobel Marshall (6)
Ramsey Manor Lower School, Barton Le Clay

Planets

P lanets are colourful, there is one near the moon, the Earth
L ight came from the sun
A rmstrong took off to the moon
N eil Armstorng was the first on the moon
E veryone knows that Neil was the one on the moon
T hey landed in a boat
S tars shooting around the planets.

Sam Dreyer (6)
Ramsey Manor Lower School, Barton Le Clay

Planets

P lanets spinning around the sun
L eaping around space
A steroids flying
N othing might live there
E normous craters on the moon
T urning planets around the sun
S olar system is multicoloured.

Ben Miller (6)
Ramsey Manor Lower School, Barton Le Clay

Planets

P lanets gliding so high in the sky
L ots of planets zooming away
A nd planets shine
N ight - the moon comes out
E agle landed on the moon in 1969
T ook them three days to walk on the moon
S o famous - Neil Armstrong.

Adam Mann (7)
Ramsey Manor Lower School, Barton Le Clay

My First Acrostic - The South

Planets

P lanets are colourful
L ight stars shine in the sky
A rmstrong is really exciting
N eil Armstrong was the first to step on the moon
E agle was his landing craft
T wisting stars in the sky
S lowly the Earth is moving.

Leanne Day (6)
Ramsey Manor Lower School, Barton Le Clay

Space

S lowly like clouds
P lanets flying around space
A stronauts go on the moon
C rew was Apollo II
E verywhere is dark.

Georgia Philpot (6)
Ramsey Manor Lower School, Barton Le Clay

Space

S un is the hottest planet of all
P lanet will make the cold, the sun will make the hot
A nd all the planets will have to stick to spinning around
C louds of the planets will have to be right up in the sky
E agle was the landing mission.

Ellie Bromhall (6)
Ramsey Manor Lower School, Barton Le Clay

Space

- **S** hiny planet flying
- **P** lanets fly around
- **A** stronauts fly by
- **C** olourful planets shine
- **E** verywhere is space.

Chloe Burr (6)
Ramsey Manor Lower School, Barton Le Clay

Space

- **S** pinning bits of glitter
- **P** lanets moving around
- **A** stronauts jump around
- **C** olourful planets spinning around
- **E** agle landed on the moon.

Oliver Mann (6)
Ramsey Manor Lower School, Barton Le Clay

Space

- **S** tars bright like on firework night
- **P** lanets in the sky going round slowly
- **A** stronauts take one giant step on the moon
- **C** rater on the moon when Eagle landed
- **E** nd of the moon is upside down.

Ben S Smart (6)
Ramsey Manor Lower School, Barton Le Clay

My First Acrostic - The South

Space

S hining with bursting colours
P lanets glide gracefully across space
A stronauts fly about in space
C old like a big orange in the sky
E agle was his craft on the moon.

Ben O Smart (6)
Ramsey Manor Lower School, Barton Le Clay

Space

S pace is like the best place
P lanets glide around the place
A pinch of glitter in the stars
C ool and dusty
E at and drink.

Aneesa Qurban (6)
Ramsey Manor Lower School, Barton Le Clay

Space

S tars slowly float around space
P lanets glow in the sky
A steroids on the moon exploding
C olourful comets in the sky
E very planet makes a picture.

Joshua Webster (6)
Ramsey Manor Lower School, Barton Le Clay

Space

- **S** now glittering around space
- **P** lanets floating around space
- **A** stronauts leaping in space
- **C** raters are massive
- **E** normous planets in space.

Oliver Holder (6)
Ramsey Manor Lower School, Barton Le Clay

Space

- **S** tars shooting in space
- **P** lane
- **A** stronauts on the moon
- **C** olourful comets
- **E** very planet makes a picture.

Blayn Gill (7)
Ramsey Manor Lower School, Barton Le Clay

Space

- **S** tars glitter in the night
- **P** lanets spinning round
- **A** stronauts floating in the sky
- **C** olourful the moon is
- **E** very day planets spin.

Ava Powell (6)
Ramsey Manor Lower School, Barton Le Clay

My First Acrostic - The South

Space

S aturn has really massive rings
P luto is really tiny and it is all water
A stronauts go zooming
C olourful planets glide around the solar system
E normous rings going around Saturn.

Taylor Watson (7)
Ramsey Manor Lower School, Barton Le Clay

Space

S parkling shimmering shiny stars floating
P lanets swirl and swirl around space
A man has gone on the moon
C omets shoot and are colourful in the sky
E verything floats in space.

Abbie Giles (6)
Ramsey Manor Lower School, Barton Le Clay

Space

S aturn has a snowy ring round it
P luto is a very, very tiny planet
A steroids float around in space
C olourful planets floating in space
E normous planets floating in space.

Milly Heys (6)
Ramsey Manor Lower School, Barton Le Clay

Space

S tars twinkle in our solar system
P luto is the coldest planet
A steroids floating in space
C omets hitting Earth
E normous planets glide through space.

Joseph Holloway (6)
Ramsey Manor Lower School, Barton Le Clay

Space

S hining stars through the night
P luto is very, very small
A is for apples shaped like Mars
C olourful planets which float around
E normous planets floating around space.

Beau Garner (6)
Ramsey Manor Lower School, Barton Le Clay

Space

S tars floating fast around the black hole
P lanets spinning in the darkness of space
A stronauts leaping through the pitch-black dark space
C rackling rockets from the dark starry sky
E normous planets twisting through the solar system.

Jonah Barton (6)
Ramsey Manor Lower School, Barton Le Clay

My First Acrostic - The South

Stars

S piky stars and glittery
T hat twinkle
A stronauts go into space
R ockets fly in space
S tars floating in space.

Lauren Elliott (7)
Ramsey Manor Lower School, Barton Le Clay

Stars

S tars are glittering in the sky
T winkle stars in the sky
A stronauts are fast in rockets zooming to the moon
R ockets fly in space
S tars float in space.

Hannah Dixon (6)
Ramsey Manor Lower School, Barton Le Clay

Space

S tars glittering, shining and whizzing across the dark sky
P lanets are colourful, some are hot and some are cold
A stronauts are jumping on the grey, dusty, hard moon
C omets whizzing and shooting through the very dark sky
E normous planets like Jupiter are very big.

Eleanor Hoyle (6)
Ramsey Manor Lower School, Barton Le Clay

Space

S parkle stars floating and shimmering in the dark

P eaceful planets spinning round the solar system

A steroid whizzing and bashing against each other

C olourful planets floating round the sun

E normous craters on the dusty round moon.

Euan Randall (6)
Ramsey Manor Lower School, Barton Le Clay

Space

S un is the hottest place in space

P eaceful, grey, dusty moon

A stronauts floating around in the darkness

C omets swirling around astronauts

E normous craters on the grey moon.

Jessica Woods (6)
Ramsey Manor Lower School, Barton Le Clay

Stars

S parkling shining little stars in space

T winkle, twinkle, all stars ever so bright

A very special twinkle in each star

R eally lovely little star

S tand ever so still so magical little thing.

Sophie Bishop (7)
Ramsey Manor Lower School, Barton Le Clay

My First Acrostic - The South

Space

S tars twinkling at night
P lanets move around
A stronauts floating around
C omets float around in space
E very planet is colourful.

Elise Rennie (6)
Ramsey Manor Lower School, Barton Le Clay

Space

S tars twinkle in the sky
P lanets are hot
A stronauts leaping on the moon
C raters are on the moon
E ven asteroids glow in space.

Grace Hattle (6)
Ramsey Manor Lower School, Barton Le Clay

Me

N ests are good
A listair is my friend
T V is brilliant
H ayley is my cousin
A pple crumble, *mmm!*
L ove is all over me
I ce cream is yummy
A pril is fun.

Nathalia Clark (7)
St Winifred's School, Portswood

Me

A pples are my favourite

L ava is hot!

I love maths

S tar Wars toys are my favourite

T imes tables is my favourite

A listair likes pasta

I love going to school

R eading is my favourite.

Alistair Howard (5)
St Winifred's School, Portswood

Me

R uns fast

U g is a monster in my book!

G iants are very big

G is a letter in my name

E is my favourite letter

R ubina comes and gets me

O h it's raining!

Ruggero Ullan Pastore (5)
St Winifred's School, Portswood

My First Acrostic - The South

Me

A utumn is my favourite season
N ine is my favourite number
K angaroo is my favourite animal
I like pizza
T imes tables is my favourite subject.

Ankit Nambiar (6)
St Winifred's School, Portswood

Me

N ight-time is for sleeping
A pples are my favourite food
O n Friday I like bringing a toy
M ummy likes doing puzzles
I like playing in the park.

Naomi Collymore (5)
St Winifred's School, Portswood

My Name

D oes have a naughty sister
O nly plays the Wii at weekends
M akes really good Lego toys
I s tall and has blonde hair
N ever wants to go to bed
I s quiet when he's playing
C omputers are his favourites.

Dominic Chatterton-Sim (7)
Shoreham College, Shoreham by Sea

My Name

L oves fish
L ike football
E ating ham, egg and chips
W alking in the woods
Y ummy Cheerios

J umping to music
O pening presents
N on-stop chatterbox
E njoys playing with cars
S uper sealife centre.

Llewellyn Jones (6)
Shoreham College, Shoreham by Sea

My Name

M ackenzie
A great name
C annon - curly c not . . .
K icking K
E ats
N othing but . . .
Z ebras and red sauce
I n the
E vening.

Mackenzie Cannon (6)
Shoreham College, Shoreham by Sea

My First Acrostic - The South

My Name

W ants to be friends with everyone
I nterested in all sports
L ives life to the full
L oves playing football
I s a chilled out kid
A lways goes to watch Brighton matches
M ust do his best.

William Huet (6)
Shoreham College, Shoreham by Sea

My Name

T houghtful and kind
H elpful to everyone
O utside in the tool shed
M akes everybody laugh
A nnoys his brother
S ometimes is a little monkey.

Thomas Wootton (6)
Shoreham College, Shoreham by Sea

My Name

S aucy and smiley
Y es, she loves to talk
D ancing fairy
N aughty but nice
E njoys her food
Y ummy cuddles.

Sydney Gillman (6)
Shoreham College, Shoreham by Sea

My Name

J oking and likes being funny
O n my best behaviour at all times
S its on the sofa and watches TV
E njoys playing on the DS
P lays tennis
H appy, good, kind and nice.

Joseph Ainsworth (6)
Shoreham College, Shoreham by Sea

My Name

J acket potatoes, beans and cheese is my favourite school dinner
O nly likes cake
S tar Wars is my best film
H air is blonde
U sually I am sensible and nice
A nd sometimes I am silly.

Joshua Stearns (6)
Shoreham College, Shoreham by Sea

My First Acrostic - The South

Witch

W atery and weary
I nky spell in her book
T urning people into frogs
C ackling with glee
H ome on her broom.

Roseanna Davey (6)
The Christian School, Takeley

Kite

K een to fly in the air
I n the wind and the breeze
T rying to fly away
E asy to see.

Rachel Fyfe (6)
The Christian School, Takeley

Seaside

S eagulls jumping in the sea
E ating yummy cold ice cream
A mazing dolphins diving into the sea
S hiny rocks on the beach
I n the sea there is lots of seaweed
D elicious hot dogs to eat
E veryone is excited when they go to the beach.

Ella-Mae Sinkia (6)
Trotts Hill Primary School, Stevenage

Autumn Walk

A corns twirl in the breeze and squirrels play with them
U nder the log sleep two little hedgehogs huddled together
T rees have lost their leaves
U nusual shaped leaves lie on the ground
M onths and months those little hedgehogs have been sleeping
N ature is a wonderful thing.

Ella Upcraft (6)
Tylers Green First School, High Wycombe

Wills Farm

W ill Loves playing with logs.
I n the farmer's field.
L oves to climb on them to see if there are birds in them.
L oves to see if there are any eggs.

Will Redmayne (7)
Whalton CE Aided First School, Morpeth

My First Acrostic - The South

Young Writers Information

We hope you have enjoyed reading this book - and that you will continue to enjoy it in the coming years.

If you like reading and writing poetry drop us a line, or give us a call, and we'll send you a free information pack.

Alternatively if you would like to order further copies of this book or any of our other titles, then please give us a call or log onto our website at www.youngwriters.co.uk.

Young Writers Information
Remus House
Coltsfoot Drive
Peterborough
PE2 9JX
(01733) 890066